woodland crochet

12 Precious Projects to Stitch and Snuggle

KRISTEN RASK

becker&mayer!
BOOK PRODUCERS

contents

Introduction . . . 3

Crochet Hook Metric Conversion Chart . . . 4

About this Kit . . . 5

Techniques and Terminology . . . 6

Project 1: Owl . . . 12

Project 2: Fox . . . 18

Project 3: Fawn . . . 24

Project 4: Beaver . . . 30

Project 5: Raccoon . . . 36

Project 6: Squirrel . . . 42

Project 7: Mouse . . . 48

Project 8: Skunk . . . 52

Project 9: Hedgehog . . . 56

Project 10: Bunny . . . 60

Project 11: Bird . . . 64

Project 12: Tortoise . . . 68

About the Author . . . 72

Acknowledgments . . . 73

Where to Find the Artists . . . 74

Introduction

Every summer when I was a kid, my parents would take my sister and me camping. Sometimes we were up in the Rockies, other times we just explored regions closer to our home in Ohio. Sometimes we enjoyed these trips, other times we complained (we were kids!). My mom pretended to not be scared of bears, my dad took life-threatening photos, and I was totally terrified. The woods are mysterious, scary, and exciting. If I put aside my fears of getting eaten by a bear or a mountain lion, I enjoyed looking at all the magical things the woods provided. And that included all the adorable animals in them.

I was really excited to create this kit because it focused on some of the cutest furry friends out there. I was lucky to work with amazing artists to create these irresistible cuddlies just for you; I hope you enjoy this kit as much as I enjoyed putting it together. Don't forget to put down the crochet hook and enjoy a little time in the woods, too.

Enjoy!

xo,
Kristen

crochet hook
Metric Conversion Chart

US	Metric (mm)
B/1	2.25
C/2	2.75
D/3	3.25
E/4	3.50
F/5	3.75
G/6	4.00
7	4.50
H/8	5.00
I/9	5.50
J/10	6.00
K/10.5	6.50
L/11	8.00
M/13	9.00
N/15	10.0

About this Kit

COMPONENTS:

This kit comes with everything you need to make two patterns in the book: the Fox and the Fawn. Included are the following components: a crochet hook, fiberfill for stuffing, a tapestry needle, four black plastic safety eyes, orange yarn, brown yarn, black yarn, white yarn, and black embroidery floss.

a

b

c

Techniques and Terminology

Before you start any of the twelve cute patterns in this kit, practice the various stitches and learn their abbreviations.

Slip Knot (sk): Every crochet project begins with a slip knot.
1. Wrap the yarn around your finger, creating a loop with a six-inch tail. **(see fig. a)**
2. Pull one end of the yarn through the loop to create a knot. The knot should be taut, but not too tight to slip your hook through. **(see fig. b and c)**

Yarn Over (yo): A basic technique that's used frequently, "yarn over" simply means to wrap the yarn over the hook.
1. With your hook in your right hand and your yarn in your left, pull the yarn around from behind the hook.
2. The strand of your "working yarn" (the yarn coming from the skein) should be across the throat of your hook on top.

Slip Stitch (sl st): This stitch is used to connect pieces, strengthen edges, or fasten off stitches.
1. Insert hook into stitch.
2. Yo and draw hook through chain and loop on hook.

Chain Stitch (ch): The foundation of any project, the chain stitch is either worked in rows or in a ring. For most of the projects in this book, you will be working in a ring.
1. To begin a chain stitch, start with a slip knot.
2. Yo, then draw yarn through the loop, making the first stitch. Continue working in this manner until you have the desired number of stitches. **(see figs. d and e)**

Working into the chain: Occasionally a pattern will say to work into the front or back of a chain. The front of the chain looks like a series of Vs, and the back of the chain has a ridge (or bump) behind each chain stitch.

Back loop only (BLO): Occasionally a pattern will ask you to work in the back loop only. When you look at your chain, you will insert your hook into the back of the loop only.
(see fig. f)

Front loop only (FLO): Occasionally a pattern will ask you to work in the front loop only. When you look at your chain, you will insert your hook into the front of the loop only.
(see fig. g—NEXT PAGE)

Single Crochet (sc):
1. Insert your hook into desired stitch.
   (see fig. h—NEXT PAGE)
2. Yo and draw yarn through the loop. You will now have two loops on your hook.
3. Yo again and draw yarn through both loops to complete a single crochet.
   (see figs. i and j—NEXT PAGE)

Adjustable Ring: Because amigurumi pieces are made mostly "in the round," the adjustable ring is the first step of many patterns and is an invaluable technique to master. An adjustable ring is used to mark where the circle begins and ends, so you can keep track of which row you're working on.
1. Chain two times (ch 2).
2. Sl st through the first stitch.
   Each pattern will then tell how many single crochets to make in the ring.

Half Double Crochet (hdc): This stitch is between single crochet and double crochet in height.
1. Yo and insert hook into the desired stitch.
2. Yo and draw yarn through the stitch, leaving three loops on your hook.
3. Yo one last time and draw yarn through all three loops.

Double Crochet (dc): The double crochet, the most commonly used stitch, is taller than the single crochet.

1. Yo first, then insert hook into a desired stitch. **(see fig. k)**
2. Yo, then draw your hook through the stitch, leaving three loops on the hook. **(see fig. l)**
3. Yo, then draw yarn through the first two loops on the hook, leaving both loops on the hook. Yo one more time and pull yarn through the two remaining loops.

Extended Half Double Crochet (ehdc):

1. Yo first, then insert hook into a desired stitch.
2. Yo, then draw your hook through the stitch, leaving three loops on the hook.
3. Yo, then draw yarn through one loop on the hook, leaving three loops on the hook.
4. Yo, then draw up the last three loops on hook. **(see fig. m—NEXT PAGE)**

Half Treble Crochet (htr): A step between the double crochet and treble crochet.

1. Yo, insert hook into desired stitch.
2. Yo, draw through loop.
3. Yo, pull through all three loops on hook.

Treble Crochet (tr): This stitch is used to make the longest stitches.

1. Yo hook two times, then insert hook into desired stitch.
2. Yo hook and draw yarn through the stitch, leaving four loops on the hook.
3. Yo and draw yarn through two loops, leaving three loops on the hook.
4. Yo and draw yarn through two loops, leaving two loops on the hook.
5. Yo and draw yarn through last two remaining loops.

DECREASING:
Invisible Decrease (invdc)

1. Insert your hook into the front stitch. **(see fig. n—NEXT PAGE)**

2. Insert hook into the front loop of the next stitch, tilt your crochet hook down to get into the stitch. **(see fig. o—NEXT PAGE)**

3. Yo, then draw yarn through the first two loops on hook **(see fig. p—NEXT PAGE)**

4. Yo, then draw yarn through last two loops on hook

Single Crochet Two Together (sc2tog): This abbreviation for decreasing means to single crochet the next two stitches together. By doing this, you will combine stitches, making the piece smaller.

1. Insert your hook into the desired stitch.

2. Yo, pull through loop.

3. Next, insert hook into the next stitch after that, leaving three loops on the hook. **(see fig. q—NEXT PAGE)**

4. Yo, then draw yarn through all three loops.

Single Crochet Three Together (sc3tog): This abbreviation for decreasing means to single crochet the next three stitches together. By doing this, you will combine stitches, making the piece smaller.

1. Insert hook into desired stitch.

2. Yo, pull through loop.

3. Insert hook into 2nd stitch.

4. Yo, pull through loop.

5. Insert hook into third stitch.

6. Yo, pull through loop.

7. Yo and pull through all four loops. **(see fig. r—NEXT PAGE)**

Front Post Double Crochet (fpdc):

1. Yo, insert hook from the front of the post, going into the back, then coming out to the front again, draw up a loop.

2. Yo and pull through two loops.

3. Yo and pull through both loops.

Back Post Double Crochet (bpdc):

1. Yo, insert hook from the back of the post, going into the front, then coming out to the back again, draw up a loop.

2. Yo and pull through two loops.

3. Yo and pull through both loops.

Half Double Crochet Together (hdc2tog): With this stitch, you make two half double crochets into one.
1. Yo, insert hook into desired stitch.
2. Pull up on loop.
3. Yo, insert hook into next stitch.
4. Pull up on loop.
5. Yo, pull through all 5 loops on hook.

Adding yarn: To change colors or start on a new skein after running out of yarn, follow these simple steps.
At the end of a row:
1. Make a slip knot with the new skein, leaving a tail.
2. Insert the hook where you are to start crocheting.
3. Continue to follow pattern.

In the middle of a row, change yarn when there are two loops left on your hook:
1. Grab old yarn together with a six-inch tail of new yarn.
2. Yo the new yarn as usual.
3. Pull through the two loops on the hook, completing the stitch.

Weave in ends: This finishing step means to sew (or "weave") yarn into a finished piece to prevent unraveling. After cutting a six-inch tail, thread yarn onto a yarn needle and weave through the back of the project's stitches. Do not go in and out of the project, as it will appear on the finished side and show.

Crochet surface chain/embroidery chain: To create designs on crocheted fabric, use slip stitches to "draw" your design:
1. Make a slip knot.
2. Attach the knot to back of your work so you can't see it through the front.
3. Remove hook from back and insert it into a stitch next to the working loop in the front from the back of work.
4. Insert hook into working loop and pull the loop through so that you are at the front of the work.

5. Begin making slip stitches with your yarn feeding from the back of your work. **(see fig. s)**

6. Insert hook into desired stitch.

7. Yo and draw through loop.

8. Continue with your design. **(see fig. t)**

9. When done, remove the hook from the working loop.

10. Insert hook from the back of your work, picking up working loop and bringing it to the back.

11. Yo and pull through loop. Finish off and weave in ends.

Hook size: At the beginning of each pattern, a desired hook size is listed. Hook sizes range from small at the beginning of the alphabet to larger as the letters go on. The hook size affects the gauge—the number of stitches in a square inch—and will determine the finished project size. Tighter stitches will ensure that stuffing won't emerge through gaps, although they should be loose enough to work through them with the hook.

Reading a pattern: The patterns in this book are mostly in rounds (rnd), meaning instead of being made in flat "rows" of stitches, they're worked in circular rows of stitches, or "rounds."

- Some crochet makers use a stitch marker to keep track of the start of each round and it is highly suggested.
- Asterisks surrounding instructions indicate that you should repeat that set of steps.

   Example: *2sc in st, 3sc*
   Translation: single crochet 2x's in same stitch and then single crochet 3x's and repeat those steps around.

- A number within parentheses following asterisked instructions indicates how many stitches should be in that round, which can be highly beneficial to those new to crochet.

   Example: *4sc, (sc2tog) 2x*
   Translation: single crochet 4xs and then single crochet 2 together 2x's and then repeat those steps around.

owl

FROM HEATHER JARMUSZ, ILLINOIS

Whoooo wouldn't love this adorable owl? Designed by Heather Jarmusz, this owl will bring a lot of joy to the owl lovers in your life. Even though most owls are known to be solitary animals, this owl loves company. You'll be addicted to making these adorable, big-eyed creatures!

what you'll need:

- Worsted weight yarn in Brown, Orange, Sage, Light Green, and White
- F/5 (3.75mm) crochet hook
- Tapestry needle
- Pair of black plastic safety eyes (12mm)
- Stuffing

FINISHED SIZE: 6" tall

Instructions

EYE PATCHES (X2): White yarn
- Make an adjustable ring.

Rnd 1: 6sc in ring (6)
Rnd 2: 2sc in each st (12)
Rnd 3: *2sc in next st, sc in next st* (18)
Rnd 4: *2sc in next st, 2sc* (24)
- Finish off, leaving long tail for sewing to face.

HEAD AND BODY: Brown yarn, Sage yarn, and Light Green yarn
- With Brown yarn, make an adjustable ring.

Rnd 1: 6sc in ring (6)
Rnd 2: 2sc in each st (12)
Rnd 3: *2sc in next st, sc in next st* (18)
Rnd 4: *2sc in next st, 2sc* (24)
Rnd 5: *2sc in next st, 3sc* (30)
Rnd 6: *2sc in next st, 4sc* (36)
Rnd 7: *2sc in next st, 5sc* (42)
Rnd 8-20: sc in each st (42)
- Position eye patches and attach safety eyes through the fabric between rounds 13 and 14. Fasten safety eyes securely.
  (see fig. 1a)

Rnd 21: *invdec over next 2 sts, 5sc* (36)
(see fig. 1b)
Rnd 22: *invdec over next 2 sts, 4sc* (30)
Rnd 23: *invdec over next 2 sts, 3sc* (24)
Rnd 24: *invdec over next 2 sts, 2sc* (18)
- Change to Sage yarn at the end of round 24. Stuff head firmly with stuffing.

Rnd 25: sc in each st (18)
Rnd 26: *2sc in next st, 2sc* (24)
- Change to Light Green yarn at the end of round 26.

Rnd 27: *2sc in next st, 3sc* (30)
Rnd 28: sc in each st (30)
- Change to Sage yarn at the end of round 28.

Rnd 29-30: sc in each st (30)
- Change to Light Green yarn at the end of round 30. **(see fig. 1c)**

Rnd 31-32: sc in each st (30)
- Change to Sage yarn at the end of round 32.

Rnd 33-34: sc in each st (30)
- Change to Light Green at the end of round 34.

Rnd 35-36: sc in each st (30)
- Change to Sage yarn at the end of round 36.

Rnd 37-38: sc in each st (30)
- Change to Light Green at the end of round 38.

Rnd 39: *invdec over next 2 sts, 3sc* (24)

Rnd 40: *invdec over next 2 sts, 2sc* (18)
- Change to Sage yarn at the end of round 40.

Rnd 41: *invdec over next 2 sts, sc in next st* (12)
- Stuff body firmly with stuffing. **(see fig. 1d)**

Rnd 42: invdec around (6)
- Finish off, closing up hole. Weave in ends.

EARS (X2): Brown yarn
- Make an adjustable ring.

Rnd 1: 4sc in ring (4)

Rnd 2: *2sc in next st, sc in next st* (6)

Rnd 3: *2sc in next st, 2sc* (8)

Rnd 4: *2sc in next st, 3sc* (10)

Rnd 5: *2sc in next st, 4sc* (12)
- Finish off, leaving a long tail for sewing to face.
- Sew ear closed **(see fig. 1e)**, then sew to the top edge of the head on either side, using photos as placement guides.

BEAK: Orange yarn
- Make an adjustable ring.

Rnd 1: 4sc in ring (4)

Rnd 2: *2sc in next st, sc in next st* (6)

Rnd 3: *2sc in next st, 2sc* (8)

Rnd 4: *2sc in next st, 3sc* (10)
- Finish off, leaving a long tail for sewing to face. Stuff lightly and sew to face, using photos as placement guides.

FEET (X2): Orange yarn
- Make an adjustable ring.

Rnd 1: 6sc in ring (6 sts).

Rnd 2: 2sc in each st (12)

Rnd 3: sc in each st (12)

Rnd 4: *invdec over next 2 sts, sc in next st* (8)

- Finish off, leaving a long tail for sewing to body.
- Sew foot closed and sew to the front of body. **(see fig. 1f)** Weave in ends.

WINGS (X2): Brown yarn

- Make an adjustable ring.

Rnd 1: 6sc in ring (6)

Rnd 2: sc in each st (6)

Rnd 3: *2 sc in next st, sc in next * around (9) **(see fig. 1g)**

Rnd 4: sc in each st (9 sts)

Rnd 5: *2 sc in next st, 2sc* (12)

Rnd 6: *2 sc in next st, 3sc* (15)

Rnd 7: *2 sc in next st, 4sc* (18)

Rnd 8: *2 sc in next st, 5sc* (21)

Rnd 9–14: sc in each st (21)

Rnd 15: *invdec over next 2 sts, 5sc* (18)

Rnd 16: *invdec over next 2 sts, 4sc* (15)

- Finish off, leaving a long tail for sewing to body.
- Sew wing closed, and sew to either side of body at round 24. Weave in ends.

fox

FROM KANDICE SORAYA GROTE, CALIFORNIA

What DOES the fox say? This fox says, "Make me, love me, and I will love you back for eternity!" Best fox ever! Designed by the lovely Kandice Soraya Grote, this little fox doesn't really need to say much. One look at that adorable face and you'll automatically reach for that crochet hook.

what you'll need:

- Worsted weight yarn in Orange, Black, and White
- F/5 (3.75mm) crochet hook
- Tapestry needle
- Pair of black plastic safety eyes (6mm) Black embroidery thread
- Stuffing

FINISHED SIZE: 3.5" tall

Instructions

HEAD: Orange yarn and White yarn
• With Orange yarn, make an adjustable ring.
Rnd 1: 7sc in ring (7)
Rnd 2: 2sc in each st (14)
Rnd 3: *sc, 2sc in next st* (21)
Rnd 4-6: sc in each st (21)
• Change to White yarn.
Rnd 7: sc in each st (21)
Rnd 8: *5sc, sc2tog* (18)
Rnd 9: *4sc, sc2tog* (15)
• Pause crocheting, attach safety eyes between rounds 5 and 6.
Rnd 10: *3sc, sc2tog* (12)
• Pause, stuff firmly.
Rnd 11: *2sc, sc2tog* (8) **(see fig. 2a)**
Rnd 12: *skip a st, sc2tog* (4)
• Stuff head with stuffing and finish off.

2a

NOSE: Orange yarn
• Make an adjustable ring.
Rnd 1: 5sc in ring (5)
Rnd 2: sc in each st (5)
• Finish off, leaving a long tail for sewing into head.
• Use black embroidery thread to sew in a nose and smile. **(see fig. 2b)**
• Place a small amount of stuffing into the nose before sewing it into the center of the head.

2b

EARS (X2): Black yarn and Orange yarn
• With Black yarn, make an adjustable ring.
Rnd 1: 5sc in ring (5)
Rnd 2: sc in each st (5)
• Change to Orange yarn.
Rnd 3: *sc, 2sc in next st* (2x), sc (7)

2c

2d

2e

Rnd 4–6: sc in each st (7)
Rnd 7: sc, sc2tog, sctog (3)
- Leaving unstuffed, finish off, leaving a long tail for sewing into head.

BODY: Orange yarn
- Make an adjustable ring.
Rnd 1: 7sc in ring (7)
Rnd 2: 2sc in each st (14)
Rnd 3: *sc, 2sc in the next st* (21)
Rnd 4–5: sc in each st (21)
Rnd 6: *3sc, sc2tog*, sc (17) **(see fig. 2c)**
Rnd 7: *2sc, sc2tog*, sc (13)
Rnd 8: *sc, sc2tog*, sc (9)
Rnd 9: *sc, sc2tog* (2x), sc (6)
- Stuff body firmly with stuffing, finish off.

ARMS (X2): Black yarn and Orange yarn
- With Black yarn, make an adjustable ring.
Rnd 1: 5sc in ring (5)
Rnd 2–4: sc in each st (5)
- Change to orange yarn. **(see fig. 2d)**
Rnd 5–6: sc in each st (5)
- Finish off, leaving a long tail for sewing, small amount of stuffing.

FEET (X2): Black yarn
- Make an adjustable ring.
Rnd 1: 5sc in ring (5)
Rnd 2–4: sc in each st (5)
- Finish off, leaving a long tail for sewing, small amount of stuffing.

TAIL: White yarn and Orange yarn
- With White yarn, make an adjustable ring.
Rnd 1: 6sc in ring (6)
Rnd 2: sc in each st (6)
Rnd 3: *sc, 2sc in the next st (9)
Rnd 4: *2sc, 2sc in the next st* (12)
Rnd 5: sc in each st (12)
- Change to Orange yarn.
Rnd 6: sc in each st. (12)

2f

Rnd 7: *4sc, sc2tog* (10)
- Pause crocheting, stuff unfinished tail firmly with stuffing. **(see fig. 2e)**

Rnd 8: *3sc, sc2tog* (8)

Rnd 9–10: sc in each st (8)

Rnd 11: *2sc, sc2tog* (6)

Rnd 12: sc in each st (6)

Rnd 13: sc, sc2tog, sc, sc (4)

- Finish off, leaving a long tail to sew into body. Complete stuffing the tail.

FINISHING:
- Weave in all ends on each body part.
- Sew the legs and tail into body. **(see fig. 2f)**
- Sew both ears to top of head.
- Finish by aligning the head to the top of the body and sewing together.

fawn

FROM RACHELLE SMITH, SALT LAKE CITY, UTAH

This little baby is taking a rest because it's hard being a fawn. Foraging for your own food can be a lot of work when you're young, so sometimes you just gotta take a nap! This beauty was designed by Rachelle Smith for you to make and love for years to come. Make a diorama with it, give it to your kid to snuggle with at night, or give it to a fawn lover in your life (we all have one!).

what you'll need:

- Worsted weight yarn in Tan, Black, and White
- F/5 (3.75mm) crochet hook
- Tapestry needle
- Pair of black plastic safety eyes (12mm) Stuffing

FINISHED SIZE: about 6" long

Instructions

HEAD: Black yarn and Tan yarn
• With Black yarn, make an adjustable ring.
Rnd 1: 3sc into ring, switch to Tan (3)
Rnd 2–3: sc in each st (3)
Rnd 4: 2sc in each st (6)
Rnd 5: 2sc in each st (12)
Rnd 6: *sc, 2sc in next st* (18)
Rnd 7: *2sc, 2sc in next st* (24) **(see fig. 3a)**
Rnd 8: sc in each st (24)
Rnd 9: *2sc, sc2tog* (18)
Rnd 10: *sc, sc2tog* (12)
• Pause crocheting, attach safety eyes between rounds 10 and 11. Stuff head with stuffing.
Rnd 11: *sc2tog* (6)
Rnd 12: *sc2tog* (3)
• Finish off, leaving a tail, and sew head closed.

BODY: Tan yarn
• Make an adjustable ring.
Rnd 1: 5sc in ring (5)
Rnd 2: 2sc in each st (10)
Rnd 3: sc in each st (10)
Rnd 4: *sc, 2sc in next st* (15)
Rnd 5: *2sc, 2sc in next st* (20)
Rnd 6: sc in each st (20)
Rnd 7: *3sc, 2sc in next st* (25)
Rnd 8–11: sc in each st
Rnd 12: *3sc, sc2tog* (20)
Rnd 13: sc in each st (20)
Rnd 14: *2sc, sc2tog* (15)
Rnd 15: sc in each st (15)
• Stuff body with stuffing.
Rnd 16: *sc, sc2tog* (10)
Rnd 17: *sc2tog* (5)
Rnd 18–19: sc in each st (5)

- Finish off, leaving a tail.
- Stuff neck with stuffing, and sew head to body.

EAR (X2): Tan yarn

Note: Done in one row around foundation chain.
- ch 6, start in 2nd ch from hook.

Row 1: 2sc, dc, sc, 2sc in next st, then continuing around the chain, sc, dc, 2sc (10) **(see fig. 3b)**
- Finish off, leaving a long tail to sew onto head.

INNER EAR (X2): White yarn
- ch 6, start in 2nd ch from hook.

Row 1: 2sc, dc, sc, sl st (4)
- Finish off, leaving a tail to sew onto outer ears.
- Sew into outer ear **(see fig. 3c)** and then sew ear to head.

LEGS (X4): Black yarn and Tan yarn
- With Black yarn, make an adjustable ring.

Rnd 1: 4sc into ring (4)
Rnd 2: sc in each st, switch to Tan (4)
Rnd 3-12: sc in each st (4)
- Finish off, leaving a long tail.

HAUNCH (X2): Tan yarn
- ch 4, start in 2nd ch from hook

Row 1: sc across, ch 1, turn (3)
Row 2: 2sc in next st, sc, 2sc in next st ch 1, turn (5)
Row 3: sc, 2sc in next st, sc, 2sc in next st, sc, ch 1, turn (7)
(see fig. 3d)
Row 4: sc, 2sc in next st, 3sc, 2sc in next st, sc, ch1, turn (9)
Row 5: sc in each st (9)
- Finish off, leaving a long tail.
- Sew haunch straight across top of a leg **(see fig. 3e)**, starting at the end of the leg. This together forms a back leg. Repeat for second back leg.
- Sew back legs to back end of body
  (see fig. 3f—NEXT PAGE), stuffing the haunches before closing.
- Line up the two remaining legs under the head and sew to the underside of the body.

3f

3g

3h

TAIL (X2): One with Tan yarn, one with White yarn
- ch 6, start in 2nd ch from hook.

Row 1: 2sc, dc, sc, sl st (4)
- Finish off, leaving a tail.
- Sew two pieces together with the Tan yarn tail, and then sew to body. **(see fig. 3g)**

FINISHING:
- With a small amount of Black yarn, sew two small "v" shapes on the outer edges of the eyes to create eyelashes.
- With about 20 inches of White yarn, sew little dashes onto the fawn's back to create the spots. Keep them spread out mainly on the lower back **(see fig. 3h)**. Now you've created a beautiful fawn!

beaver

FROM HEATHER JARMUSZ, ILLINOIS

If you are looking to build a new home or a dam in your backyard, sadly, this guy isn't going to be much of use to you. BUT this little beaver, designed by Heather Jarmusz, is great if you are looking for some extra cuddles in your household. This little beaver will be a loyal friend for years to come.

what you'll need:

- Worsted weight yarn in Medium Brown, Dark Brown, Beige, Black, and White
- F/5 (3.75 mm) crochet hook
- Tapestry needle
- Pair of black plastic safety eyes (12mm)
- Felt in Black, White, and Beige
- Stitch marker
- Stuffing
- Fabric glue (optional)

FINISHED SIZE: 4" tall

Instructions

HEAD AND BODY: Medium Brown yarn
- Make an adjustable ring.

Rnd 1: 6sc in ring (6)

Rnd 2: 2sc in each st (12)

Rnd 3: *2sc in next st, sc in next st* (18)

Rnd 4: *2sc in next st, 2sc* (24)

Rnd 5: *2sc in next st, 3sc* (30)

Rnd 6–11: sc in each st (30)

- Pause crocheting, attach safety eyes between rounds 6 and 7. Fasten eyes securely. **(see fig. 4a)**

Rnd 12: *2sc in next st, 4sc* (36)

Rnd 13: *2sc in next st, 5sc* (42)

Rnd 14–21: sc in each st (42)

Rnd 22: *invdec over next 2 sts, 5sc* (36)

Rnd 23: *invdec over next 2 sts, 4sc* (30)
(see fig. 4b)

Rnd 24: *invdec over next 2 sts, 3sc* (24)

Rnd 25: *invdec over next 2 sts, 2sc* (18)

Rnd 26: *invdec over next 2 sts, 1sc* (12)

Rnd 27: *invdec over next 2 sts (6)

- Stuff head and body firmly with stuffing. Finish off, closing up hole, and weave in ends.

EARS (X2): Medium Brown yarn
- Make an adjustable ring.

Rnd 1: 6sc in ring (6)

Rnd 2–3: sc in each st (6)

- Finish off, leaving long tail. Sew ears to top of beaver's head, weave in ends. **(see fig. 4c)**

ARMS (X2): Medium Brown yarn
- Make an adjustable ring.

Rnd 1: 6sc in ring (6)

Rnd 2: 2sc in each st (12)

4d

4e

4f

4g

Rnd 3: *2sc in next st, 3 sc* (15)

Rnd 4: sc in each st (15)

Rnd 5: *invdec over next 2 sts, 3sc (12)

Rnd 6: *invdec over next 2 sts, 2sc (9)

Rnd 7–12: sc in each st (9)

- Finish off, leaving long tail for sewing to body. Cut out claws from Beige felt and sew to edge of the paw using Beige yarn (or glue with fabric glue). **(see fig. 4d and 4e)**

FEET (X2): Medium Brown yarn

- Make an adjustable ring.

Rnd 1: 6sc in ring (6)

Rnd 2: 2sc in each st (12)

Rnd 3: *2sc in next st, sc in next st* (18)

Rnd 4: sc in each st (18)

Rnd 5: *invdec over next 2 sts, 1sc (12)

Rnd 6: sc in each st (12)

- Finish off, leaving long tail for sewing to body. Cut out claws from Beige felt and sew to edge of the feet using Beige yarn (or glue with fabric glue).

SNOUT: Beige yarn

- Make an adjustable ring.

Rnd 1: 6sc in ring (6)

Rnd 2: 2sc in each st (12)

Rnd 3: *2sc in next st, 3 sc* (15)

Rnd 4: sc in each st (15)

- Finish off, leaving long tail for sewing to body. Cut out triangle-shaped nose from Black felt and sew to front of snout using Black yarn **(see fig. 4f)**. Cut two teeth from White felt and sew to lower edge of snout with White yarn.

- Stuff lightly and sew snout to front of face, weave in ends.

TAIL: Dark Brown yarn

The tail is worked in an alternating [sc in next st, dc in next st] pattern.

- Make an adjustable ring.

Rnd 1: Work (sc, dc, sc, dc, sc, dc) in ring (6)

Rnd 2: Work (sc, dc) in each st (12) **(see fig. 4g)**

Rnd 3: *(sc, dc) in next st, sc in next st* (18)

Rnds 4–10: *sc in next st, dc in next st* (18)

If you end a round on a sc, start the next round with a sc. If you end a round on a dc, start the next round with a dc. This will create staggering between the scs and dcs of each round.

Rnd 11: *invdec over next 2 sts, dc in next st* (12)

Rnd 12: *sc in next st, dc in next st* (12)

- Finish off, leaving a long tail for sewing to body. Fold tail in half and whipstitch closed. **(see fig. 4h)**

FINISHING:

- Sew tail to body close to the bottom, centered on the beaver's back. Weave in ends.

raccoon

FROM KANDICE SORAYA GROTE, MERCED, CALIFORNIA

Raccoons are super-adorable but can really do a number on you if you get too close. Luckily, this raccoon, designed by Kandice Soraya Grote, is a very tender soul. Soon you will realize you have made an entire family and that they find adventure no matter where they are! Watch out, friends, this little bandit will steal your hearts away!

what you'll need:

- Worsted weight yarn in Black and Gray
- F/5 (3.75mm) crochet hook
- Tapestry needle
- Pair of black plastic safety eyes (6mm)
- Black embroidery thread
- Felt in Black and Gray
- Craft glue
- Stuffing

FINISHED SIZE: 3.5" tall

Instructions

For the mask, pre-cut two white ovals (approx. 2.5cm in diameter), and two black ovals (approx. 2cm in diameter). Make a small hole in both sets of ovals for the safety eyes. Add a little glue to keep the sides of the ovals in place.

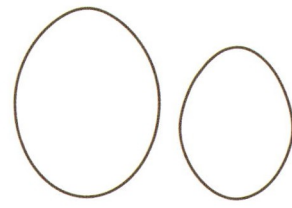

HEAD: Gray yarn
- Make an adjustable ring.

Rnd 1: 7sc in ring (7)
Rnd 2: 2sc in each st (14)
Rnd 3: *sc, 2sc in the next st* (21)
Rnd 4–7: sc in each st (21)
Rnd 8: *5sc, sc2tog* (18)
Rnd 9: *4sc, sc2tog* (15)
- Pause crocheting. Attach felt mask and safety eyes with embroidery thread between rounds 6 and 7. **(see fig. 5a)**

Rnd 10: *3sc, sc2tog* (12)
- Pause, stuff firmly.

Rnd 11: *2sc, sc2tog* (8)
Rnd 12: *sc, sc2tog* (4)
- Stuff with stuffing and finish off.

5a

NOSE: Gray yarn
- Make an adjustable ring.

Rnd 1: 5sc in ring (5)
Rnd 2: sc in each st (5)
- Finish off, leaving a long tail for sewing into head.
- Use Black embroidery thread to sew in a nose and smile. **(see fig. 5b)**
- Place a small amount of stuffing into the nose before placing it in the center of the head and sewing into place.

5b

5c

5d

5e

EARS (X2): Black yarn and Gray yarn
- With Black yarn, make an adjustable ring.

Rnd 1: 6sc in ring (6)

Rnd 2: sc in each st (6) **(see fig. 5c)**
- Change to Gray yarn.

Rnd 3: *sc, 2sc in the next st* (9)

Rnd 4: sc in each st (9)
- Leaving unstuffed, finish off, leaving a long tail for sewing into head.

BODY: Gray yarn
- Make an adjustable ring.

Rnd 1: 7sc in ring (7)

Rnd 2: 2sc in each st (14)

Rnd 3: *sc, 2sc in the next st* (21)

Rnd 4-5: sc in each st (21)

Rnd 6: *3sc, sc2tog*, sc (17) **(see fig. 5d)**

Rnd 7: *2sc, sc2tog*, sc (13)

Rnd 8: *sc, sc2tog*, sc (9)

Rnd 9: *sc, sc2tog* (2x), sc (6)
- Stuff body firmly with stuffing, finish off.

ARMS (X2): Black yarn and Gray yarn
- With Black yarn, make an adjustable ring.

Rnd 1: 5sc in ring (5)

Rnd 2-4: sc in each st (5)
- Change to Gray yarn.

Rnd 5: sc in each st (5) **(see fig. 5e)**
- Finish off, leaving a long tail for sewing, small amount of stuffing.

Rnd 6: sc in each st (5)

FEET (X2): Black yarn
- Make an adjustable ring.

Rnd 1: 5sc in ring (5)

Rnd 2-4: sc in each st (5)
- Finish off, leaving a long tail for sewing, small amount of stuffing.

TAIL: Black yarn and Gray yarn
- With Gray yarn, make adjustable ring.

Rnd 1: 6sc in ring (6)

Rnd 2: sc in each st (6)
Rnd 3: *sc, 2sc in the next st (9)
• Change to Black yarn.
Rnd 4: *2sc, 2sc in the next st* (9)
Rnd 5: sc in each st (12)
• Change to Gray yarn.
Rnd 6: sc in each st (12)
• Change to Black yarn.
Rnd 7: *4sc, sc2tog* (10)
• Change to Gray yarn.
• Pause crocheting, stuff firmly.
Rnd 8: *3sc, sc2tog* (8)
• Change to Black yarn. **(see fig. 5f)**
Rnd 9: sc in each st (8)
• Change to Gray yarn.
Rnd 10: sc in each st (8)
• Change to Black yarn.
Rnd 11: *2sc, sc2tog* (6)
Rnd 12: sc in each st (6)
Rnd 13: sc, sc2tog, sc, sc (4)
• Finish stuffing, leaving a long tail
  to sew to body.

FINISHING:
• Weave in all ends.
• Sew the arms, legs, and tail to
  body. **(see fig. 5g)**
• Sew both ears to top of head.
• Finish by aligning the head to
  the top of the body and sewing
  together.

squirrel

FROM ALICIA KACHMAR, PENNSYLVANIA

While they are adorable, city squirrels have no qualms about running up your leg to steal your burrito. When I saw this adorable squirrel designed by Alicia Kachmar, though, I thought, "Now this is a squirrel I can get behind." Adorable, friendly, AND it's already occupied with its own acorn, so I can eat my burrito in peace.

what you'll need:

- Worsted weight yarn in Gray, Olive Green, Black, and Tan
- Bulky weight yarn in Off-White
- G/6 (4.25mm) and K/10.5 (6.5mm) crochet hooks
- Tapestry needle
- Needle-felting needle
- Pair of black plastic safety eyes (8mm)
- Wool roving in Gray
- Stuffing
- Fabric glue (optional)

FINISHED SIZE: 5.5" tall

Instructions

ACORN BASE: Green yarn
- Using G hook, ch 2, start in 2nd ch from hook.

Rnd 1: 4sc (4)
Rnd 2: 2sc in each st (8)
Rnd 3: 2sc in first st, 7sc (9)
Rnd 4: sc in each st (9)
Rnd 5: *sc2tog, sc* and sl to next st, (6)
- Finish off, weave in ends.

ACORN TOP: Tan yarn
- Using G hook and leaving a long tail, ch 2, start in 2nd ch from hook.

Rnd 1: 4sc (4)
Rnd 2: 2sc in each st (8)
Rnd 3: *2sc in first st, sc in next st*, sl to next st, finish off leaving a long tail (12)
- To make stem, pull up first long tail through the center, ch 3, sc in 2nd and 3rd ch from hook, sl st into round 1, finish off.
  (see fig. 6a)

BODY: Gray yarn
- Using G hook, ch 2, start in 2nd ch from hook.

Rnd 1: 5sc (5)
Rnd 2: 2sc in each st (10)
Rnd 3: *2sc in next st, sc* (15)
Rnd 4: sc in each st (15)
Rnd 5: *2sc in next st, 2sc* (20)
Rnd 6: sc in each st (20)
Rnd 7: *2sc in st, 3sc* (25)
Rnd 8–10 : sc in each st (25)
Rnd 11: *sc2tog, 3sc* (20)
Rnd 12: sc in each st (20)
Rnd 13: *sc2tog, 3sc* (16) **(see fig. 6b)**

6c

6d

6e

Rnd 14: sc in each st (16)
Rnd 15: *sc2tog, 2sc* (12)
- Stuff body with stuffing and finish off, leaving an 8-inch tail for sewing.

EARS (X2): Gray yarn
- Using G hook, ch 3, start in 2nd ch from hook.

Rnd 1: ehdc in 2nd and 3rd ch from hook, ch 1 and sl to first ch (3) **(see fig. 6c)**
- Finish off, leaving a 4-inch tail for sewing.

NOSE: Black yarn
- Using G hook, ch 2.

Rnd 1: sl in first ch (1)
- Finish off, leaving a 4-inch tail for sewing.

HEAD: Gray yarn
- Using G hook, ch 2, start in 2nd ch from hook.

Rnd 1: 3sc (3)
Rnd 2: 2sc in each st (6)
Rnd 3: sc in each st (6)
Rnd 4: *2sc in next st, sc* (9)
Rnd 5: sc in each st (9)
Rnd 6: *2sc in next st, 2sc* (12)
Rnd 7: *2sc in next st, 3sc* (15)
Rnd 8: *2sc in next st, 4sc* (18)
Rnd 9: sc in each st (18)
Rnd 10: *sc2tog, 4sc* (15) **(see fig. 6d)**
Rnd 11: *sc2tog, sc* (10)
- Pause crocheting. Sew on nose and ears, and attach safety eyes between rounds 6 and 7. Stuff head with stuffing.

Rnd 12: *sc2tog* and sl st across (5)
- Finish off, leaving a tail for sewing.

ARMS (X2): Gray yarn
- Using G hook, ch 2, start in 2nd ch from hook.

Rnd 1: 3sc (3)
Rnd 2–8: sc in each st (3)
- Finish off, leaving a 4-inch tail for sewing.

FEET BOTTOMS (X2): Gray yarn
- Using G hook, ch 2, start in 2nd ch from hook.

Rnd 1: ch 2, 5sc in 2nd ch from hook (5)
Rnd 2: 2sc in first st, sc in each st (6)
Rnd 3–4: sc in each st (6)
Rnd 5: sc2tog, 4sc (5) **(see fig. 6e)**
Rnd 6: sl st across to opposite side
- Finish off, leaving a 4-inch tail for sewing.

LEGS (X2): Gray yarn
- Using G hook, ch 2, start in 2nd ch from hook.

Rnd 1: 6sc (6)
Rnd 2: 2sc in each st (12)
Rnd 3–6: sc in each st (12)
Rnd 7: *sc2tog, 2sc* (9)
- Stuff legs with stuffing, and finish off, leaving a 12-inch tail for sewing.

BELLY: Off-White yarn
- With Off-White yarn, using K hook, ch 3, start in 2nd ch from hook.

Row 1: sc in 2nd and 3rd ch from

6f

6g

6h

hook, ch 1, turn (2)

Row 2: sc in each st, ch 1, turn (2)

Row 3: 2sc in first st, sc, ch 1, turn (3)

Row 4: sc in each st, ch 1, turn (3)

Row 5: sc2tog, sc, ch 1, turn (2) **(see fig. 6f)**

Row 6-7: sc in each st, ch 1, turn (2)

Row 8: sc2tog, ch 1 (1)

- sc around entire belly, making 2sc in row 1, sl st to original sc made here. **(see fig. 6g)**
- Finish off, leaving a 10-inch tail for sewing.

FINISHING:

- Stuff acorn bottom and sew on top.
- Sew belly piece to body, sew on feet bottoms to legs, allowing half of foot to stick out from leg.
- Sew each leg and each arm to the sides of the body, sew head to body.
- Stretch out a 6-inch by 3-inch piece of roving. Using felting needle, tack roving down to the backside of the body. **(see fig. 6h)**
- With extra yarn or glue, attach acorn to ends of each arm.

mouse

FROM JANENE SCHOLZ, DALLAS, TEXAS

Some people scream when they see a mouse. Some people
keep them as pets. No matter what, you can't argue with
the fact that they are pretty adorable. This sweet little
guy by Janene Scholz will turn anyone into a mouse lover!
His cute little face and cuddly coat will win over even the
haters! Guaranteed!

**what
you'll
need:**

- Bulky weight yarn in Chocolate
- Worsted weight yarn in Dusty Rose
- G/6 (4.00mm) crochet hook
- Tapestry needle
- Pair of black plastic safety eyes (9mm)
- Stuffing

FINISHED SIZE: 10" long

Instructions

BODY: Chocolate yarn
- Make an adjustable ring.

Rnd 1: 6sc in ring (6)
Rnd 2: sc in each st (6)
Rnd 3: 2sc in each st (12)
Rnd 4: *sc, 2sc in next st* (18)
Rnd 5-14: sc in each st (18)
Rnd 15: *sc, sc2tog* (12) **(see fig. 7a)**
Rnd 16-17: sc in each st (12)
- Stuff body with stuffing.

Rnd 18: *sc2tog* (6)
- Finish off, leaving a long tail.

HEAD: Chocolate yarn
- Make an adjustable ring.

Rnd 1: 6sc in ring (6)
Rnd 2: sc in each st (6)
Rnd 3: 2sc in each st (12)
Rnd 4-7: sc in each st
- Attach safety eyes between rounds 4 and 5. **(see fig. 7b)**

Rnd 8: sc in each st (12)
- Stuff head with stuffing.

Rnd 9: *sc2tog* (6)
- Finish off, leaving a long tail.

EAR (X2): Dusty Rose yarn
- Make an adjustable ring.

Rnd 1: 5sc in ring (5)
Rnd 2: 2sc in each st (10) **(see fig. 7c)**
Rnd 3: *sc, 2sc in next st* (15)
Rnd 4: sc in each st (15)
- Finish off, leaving a long tail.

TAIL: Dusty Rose yarn
- ch 25

7d

7e

7f

7g

Rnd 1: 25sc (25) **(see fig. 7d)**
• Finish off, leaving a long tail.

FRONT LEG (X2): Chocolate yarn
and Dusty Rose yarn
• With Chocolate yarn, make an
  adjustable ring.
Rnd 1: 5sc in ring (5)
Rnd 2–3: sc in each st (5)
• Change to Dusty Rose yarn.
  (see fig. 7e)
Rnd 4–10: sc in each st (5)
Rnd 11: (sc2tog) 3x
• Finish off, leaving a tail.

BACK LEG (X2): Chocolate yarn and Dusty Rose yarn
• With Chocolate yarn, make an adjustable ring.
Rnd 1: 7sc in ring (7)
Rnd 2–4: sc in each st (7)
• Change to Dusty Rose yarn.
Rnd 5–11: sc in each st (7)
• Finish off, leaving a long tail, then sew the opening of foot closed.
  (see fig. 7f)

FINISHING:
• Using Dusty Rose yarn, embroider nose on head. **(see fig. 7g)**
• Sew on head, front legs, back legs, and tail.
• Weave in ends.

skunk

FROM DENISE FERGUSON, PENNSYLVANIA

These stinky little creatures are usually to be avoided, but let me introduce you to the best skunk in town. Designed by Denise Ferguson, this little creature keeps it clean. Not only does this guy not smell, but his claws are soft so he won't try to den up in the corner of your couch. Even though their counterparts in the wild are mostly solitary animals, make a whole family of skunks to love and share!

what you'll need:

- Worsted weight yarn in White, Black, and Pink
- G/6 (4.00mm) crochet hook
- Tapesty needle
- Pair of black plastic safety eyes (9mm)
- Stuffing

FINISHED SIZE: 6" long

Instructions

LEGS (X4): Black yarn
- Make an adjustable ring.

Rnd 1: 6sc in ring (6)

Rnd 2: sc in each st (6)

Rnd 3: sc in each st (6)

Rnd 4: sc in each st (6)
- Finish off, leaving a long tail to sew onto body.

EARS (x2): Black yarn
- Make an adjustable ring.

Rnd 1: 3sc in ring (3)
- Finish off, leaving a long tail to sew onto body.

BODY: Black yarn
- Make an adjustable ring.

Rnd 1: 6sc in ring (6)

Rnd 2: sc in each st (6)

Rnd 3: *sc, 2sc in next st* (9) **(see fig. 8a)**

Rnd 4–5: sc in each st (9)

Rnd 6: 2sc in each st (18)

Rnd 7–8: sc in each st (18)
- Pause crocheting. Stitch on nose with Pink yarn, attach safety eyes between rounds 5 and 6, sew on ears between rounds 7 and 8, and stitch on eyelashes with White yarn. **(see fig. 8b)**

Rnd 9: *sc, sc2tog* (12)

Rnd 10: *sc, 2sc in next st* (18)

Rnd 11: *2sc, 2sc in next st* (24)

Rnd 12–21: sc in each st (24)

Rnd 22: *2sc, sc2tog* (18)

Rnd 23: *sc, sc2tog* (12)

Rnd 24: sc2tog around (6) **(see fig. 8c)**
- Finish off and weave in ends.

8a

8b

8c

8d

8e

8f

BODY STRIPE: White yarn and Black yarn
- With White yarn, ch 2, start in 2nd ch from hook.

Row 1: sc, ch 1, turn (1)
Row 2: sc, ch 1, turn (1)
Row 3: 2sc in each st, ch 1, turn (2)
Row 4: 2sc in each st, ch 1, turn (4)
(see fig. 8d)
Row 5: sc in each st, ch 1, turn (4)
Row 6: 2sc in first st, 2sc, 2sc in next st, ch 1, turn (6)
Row 7–21: sc in each st, ch 1, turn (6)
- Finish off.
- Starting at row 1, pull a loop of Black yarn with your hook from the underside to the topside in the spaces between the rows of the stripe. Repeat to draw another loop into and through the first. Repeat until you reach the end of the stripe, and sew stripe onto body. **(see fig. 8e)**

TAIL: Black yarn
- Make an adjustable ring.

Rnd 1: 6sc in ring (6)
Rnd 2: sc in each st (6)
Rnd 3: *2sc, 2sc in next st* (8)
Rnd 4: *sc, 2sc in next st* (12)
Rnd 5: sc in each st (12)
Rnd 6: *sc, 2sc in next st* (18)
Rnd 7–15: sc in each st (18)
Rnd 16: *sc, sc2tog* (12)
- Finish off, leaving a long tail to sew onto body.

TAIL STRIPE: White yarn and Black yarn

- With White yarn, ch 2, start in 2nd ch from hook.

Row 1: sc, ch 1, turn (1)
Row 2: 2sc in each st, ch 1, turn (2)
Row 3: 2sc in each st, ch 1, turn (4)
Row 4: 2sc in first st, sc in next 2 st, 2ch in next st, ch 1, turn (6)
(see fig. 8f)
Row 5–16: sc in each st, ch 1, turn (6)
- Finish off.
- Starting at row 1, pull a loop of Black yarn with your hook from the underside to the topside in the spaces between the rows of the stripe. Repeat to draw another loop into and through the first. Repeat until you reach the end of the stripe, and sew stripe onto tail.

FINISHING:
Sew tail onto the end of the body, matching up the white stripe. Sew all 4 legs onto the underside of the body. Weave in ends. **(see fig. 8g)**

hedgehog

FROM AMANDA LYNN WILHITE, WISCONSIN

How can someone resist an adorable little hedgehog? Seriously! They are tiny little creatures with prickly little spikes coming out of their bodies, and they seem to have a perpetual expression on their faces that say, "Love me ... please." The best part of this cutie, designed by Amanda Lynn Wilhite, is that it won't prick you. Plus, it requires very little maintenance!

what you'll need:

- Worsted weight yarn in Light Brown, Beige, and Dark Brown
- Fun Fur yarn in Brown
- F/5 (3.75mm) crochet hook
- Tapestry needle
- Pair of black plastic safety eyes (6mm
- Stuffing

FINISHED SIZE: 5" long and 3" in width and height

Instructions

BODY: Light Brown yarn, Beige yarn, Dark Brown yarn, and Brown Fun Fur yarn
- With Light Brown yarn, make an adjustable ring.

Rnd 1: 6sc into ring (6)

Rnd 2: *sc, 2sc in next st * (9) **(see fig. 9a)**

Rnd 3: sc in each st (9)

Rnd 4: *2sc, 2sc in next st* (12)

Rnd 5: 2sc in next 10 st, leave 2 loops on hook in last st and change to Beige yarn, sc in each of last 2 st (22) **(see fig. 9b)**

Rnd 6–8: sc around, leave 2 loops on hook in last st to change to Brown Fun Fur yarn (22)
- Pause crocheting, attach safety eyes between rounds 5 and 6 **(see fig. 9c)** and stitch nose on face **(see fig. 9d—NEXT PAGE)** with Dark Brown yarn.

Rnd 9–21: sc in each st (22)

Rnd 22: sc2tog, 18 sc, sc2tog (20)

Rnd 23: *2sc, sc2tog* (15)
- Stuff body with stuffing.

Rnd 24: *sc, sc2tog* (10)

Rnd 25: *sc2tog* (5) **(see fig. 9e—NEXT PAGE)**
- Finish off and weave in ends.

EARS (X2): Light Brown yarn
- Make an adjustable ring.

Rnd 1: 6sc into ring (6)
- Finish off, leaving tail to sew ears partially closed. **(see fig. 9f—NEXT PAGE)**

FEET (X4): Beige yarn
- Make an adjustable ring.

Rnd 1: 5sc into ring (5)

Rnd 2: sc in each st (5)
- Finish off, leaving a long tail.

9d

9e

9f

FINISHING:

- Sew ears to head end of body.
- Sew feet to bottom of body.
  (see fig. 9g)
- Weave in ends.

9g

bunny

FROM DENISE FERGUSON, PENNSYLVANIA

This little bunny, designed by Denise Ferguson of Yummy Pancake, is the kind of bunny that won't dig up your garden looking for all the carrots. Well-behaved, well-groomed, and a super pet, this bunny will make you fall in love. Make a whole family with color changes and fun additions. You will be addicted to whipping up this guy in no time!

what you'll need:

- Worsted weight yarn in Brown
- G/6 (4.0mm) crochet hook
- Tapestry Needle
- Pair of black plastic safety eyes (9mm)
- Black plastic safety nose (10mm)
- Stuffing

FINISHED SIZE: 8.5" tall

Instructions

EARS (X2): Brown yarn
- ch 2, start in 2nd ch from hook.

Rnd 1: 6sc (6) **(see fig. 10a)**

Rnd 2: 2sc in each st (12)

Rnd 3–9: sc in each st (12)

Rnd 10: *sc2tog* around (6)
- Finish off, leaving a long tail to sew ears onto head.

TAIL: Brown yarn
- ch 2, start in 2nd ch from hook.

Rnd 1: 6sc (6)

Rnd 2: 2sc in each st (12)

Rnd 3–4: sc in each st (12)

Rnd 5: *sc2tog* (6)
- Stuff tail with stuffing and finish off, leaving a long tail to sew tail onto body.

ARMS (X2): Brown yarn
- ch 2, start in 2nd ch from hook.

Rnd 1: 5sc (5)

Rnd 2: 2sc in each st (10)

Rnd 3–11: sc in each st (10) **(see fig. 10b)**

Rnd 12: *sc2tog* (5)
- Stuff arms with stuffing and finish off, leaving a long tail to sew arms onto body.

LEGS (X2): Brown yarn
- ch 2, start in 2nd ch from hook.

Rnd 1: 5sc (5)

Rnd 2: 2sc in each st (10)

Rnd 3–13: sc in each st (10)

Rnd 14: *sc2tog* (5)
- Stuff legs with stuffing and finish off, leaving a long tail to sew legs onto body.

10a

10b

10c

10d

10e

HEAD: Brown yarn

• ch 2, start in 2nd ch from hook.

Rnd 1: 6sc (6)

Rnd 2: 2sc in each st (12)

Rnd 3: *sc, 2sc in next st* (18)

Rnd 4: *2sc, 2sc in next st* (24) **(see fig. 10c)**

Rnd 5: *3sc, 2sc in next st* (30)

Rnd 6: *4sc, 2sc in next st* (36)

Rnd 7–11: sc in each st (36)

• Pause crocheting and sew the ears onto the top of the head (be sure to flatten them before you sew them on). **(see fig. 10d)**

• Attach safety eyes between rounds 8 and 9, attach nose between rounds 10 and 11.

Rnd 12: *4sc, (sc2tog) (30)

Rnd 13: *3sc, (sc2tog) (24)

Rnd 14: *2sc, (sc2tog) (18)

Rnd 15: *sc, (sc2tog) (12)

Rnd 16: *sc2tog* around (6)

• Stuff head with stuffing and finish off, leaving a long tail to sew onto body.

BODY: Brown yarn

• ch 2, start in 2nd ch from hook.

Rnd 1: 6sc (6)

Rnd 2: 2sc in each st (12)

Rnd 3: *sc, 2sc in next st* (18)

Rnd 4: *2sc, 2sc in next st* (24)

Rnd 5: *3sc, 2sc in next st* (30)

Rnd 6–17: sc in each st (30)

Rnd 18: *3sc, (sc2tog) 2x* (24)

Rnd 19: *2sc, (sc2tog) 2x* (18) **(see fig. 10e)**

Rnd 20: *sc, (sc2tog) 2x* (12)

Rnd 21: *sc2tog* (6)

10f

• Finish off, leaving a long tail, and stuff body with stuffing. Weave in ends.

FINISHING:

• Sew the head onto top of body, and then sew arms, legs, and tail onto body. **(see fig. 10f)**

• Awesome idea: instead of sewing on the head, arms, and legs, get yourself some plastic safety joints and make this little guy jointed!

bird

FROM AMANDA LYNN WILHITE, WISCONSIN

Amanda's spirit animal is a swan, so it seemed only logical that she design one of the winged animals in this kit. This little mama bird is watching over her little babies until they are all hatched. Once you start making these, you'll start designing your own color patterns, and soon will have a whole flock (and perhaps a baker's dozen, as well)!

what you'll need:

- Worsted weight yarn in Blue, White, and Yellow
- Bulky yarn in Brown
- E/4 (3.5mm), F/5 (3.75mm), and I/9 (5.5mm) crochet hooks
- Tapestry needle
- 2 pairs of black plastic safety eyes (4mm and 6mm)
- Stuffing

FINISHED SIZE: Mama Bird: 3" tall and 2.5" wide, Baby Birdie and Eggs: 1" tall and .5" wide, Nest: 3" in diameter

Instructions

MAMA BIRD

HEAD: Blue yarn, White yarn, and Yellow yarn

- With Blue yarn, using F hook, make an adjustable ring.

Rnd 1: 6sc into ring (6)

Rnd 2: 2sc in each st (12)

Rnd 3: *sc, 2sc in next st* (18)

Rnd 4: *2sc, 2sc in next st* (24)

Rnd 5–7: sc in each st. Leave 2 loops on hook in last st to change to White yarn. (24)

Rnd 8–10: sc in each st (24) **(see fig. 11a)**

- Attach the 6mm safety eyes, between rounds 7 and 8, and stitch the beak between rounds 7 and 10 with the Yellow yarn.

Rnd 11: *2sc, sc2tog* (18) **(see fig. 11b)**

- Stuff the body with stuffing.

Rnd 12: *sc, sc2tog* (12)

Rnd 13: *sc2tog* (6)

- Finish off, leaving a long tail to make the loops on the top of the head.
- Using your pinky finger, pull the yarn tail up through the top of the bird's head over your finger through the bottom of the bird's head repeating 3 times for 3 loops. **(see fig. 11c)**
- Weave in ends.

BODY: Blue yarn

- Using F hook, make an adjustable ring.

Rnd 1: 7sc into ring (7)

Rnd 2: 2sc in each st (14)

Rnd 3–5: sc in each st (14)

Rnd 6: *sc, sc2tog* 4x, 2sc (10)

(see fig. 11d—NEXT PAGE)

- Finish off, leaving a long tail.
- Sew bird's feet with Yellow yarn.
- Stuff body with stuffing and sew to head.

11d

11e

11f

WINGS (X2): Blue yarn
- Using F hook, make an adjustable ring.

Rnd 1: 6sc into ring (6)
Rnd 2: 2sc in each of next 3 sts, leave last 3 st unworked (9)
(see fig. 11e)
- Finish off, leaving a long tail.

TAIL: Blue yarn
- Using F hook, make an adjustable ring

Rnd 1: 5sc into ring (5)
Rnd 2: 2sc in each st (10)
Rnd 3: sc in each st (10)
- Finish off, leaving a tail for sewing.
- Sew end closed and sew to body.

BABY BIRDIE: Blue yarn
- Using E hook, make an adjustable ring.

Rnd 1: 6sc into ring (6)
Rnd 2: *sc, 2sc in next st* (9)
Rnd 3-4: sc in each st (9)
- Attach the 4mm safety eyes between rounds 2 and 3, and center beak between the eyes and sew with Yellow yarn. Stuff body with stuffing. **(see fig. 11f)**

Rnd 5: *sc, sc2tog* (6)
- Finish off and weave in ends.

BABY BIRDIE WINGS (X2):
Blue yarn
- Using E hook, make an adjustable ring.

Rnd1: 5sc into ring (5)
- Finish off, leaving a tail to sew to baby birdie. **(see fig. 11g)**

11g

EGGS (X2): White yarn
- Using E hook, make an adjustable ring.

Rnd 1: 6sc into ring (6)
Rnd 2: *sc, 2sc in next st* (9)
Rnd 3-4: sc in each st (9)
- Stuff egg with stuffing.

Rnd 5: *sc, sc2tog* (6)

NEST: Brown yarn
- Using I hook, make an adjustable ring.

Rnd 1: 6sc into ring (6)
Rnd 2: 2sc in each st (12)
Rnd 3: *sc, 2sc in next st* (18)
Rnd 4: *2sc, 2sc in next st* (24)
Rnd 5: *3sc, 2sc in next st* (30)
Rnd 6-8: sc in each st (30)
- Finish off and weave in ends.

tortoise

FROM DENISE FERGUSON, PENNSYLVANIA

his tortoise, designed by Denise Ferguson, will live for years, just like his wild counterpart. But this guy has a soft shell, improving his snuggle capabilities. And unlike his wild counterpart, he is very social and enjoys the company of family and friends.

what you'll need:

- Worsted weight yarn in Green and Bright Green
- G/6 (4.25mm) crochet hook
- Tapestry needle
- Pair of black plastic safety eyes (9mm)
- Stuffing

FINISHED SIZE: 7" long

Instructions

SHELL SPOTS (X7): Green yarn
- Make an adjustable ring.

Rnd 1: 6sc in ring (6)

Rnd 2: 2sc in each st (12)

Rnd 3: *sc, 2sc in next st* (18) **(see fig. 12a)**
- Finish off, leaving a long tail to sew onto the shell.

SHELL TOP: Bright Green yarn
- ch 6, start in 2nd ch from hook.

Rnd 1: sc, 3sc, 3sc in next ch **(see fig. 12b)**, 3sc, 2sc in next ch (12)

Rnd 2: *sc, 2sc in next st* (18)

Rnd 3: *2sc, 2sc in next st* (24)

Rnd 4: *3sc, 2sc in next st* (30)

Rnd 5: *4sc, 2sc in next st* (36)

Rnd 6: *5sc, 2sc in next st* (42)

Rnd 7: *6sc, 2sc in next st* (48)

Rnd 8: *7sc, 2sc in next st* (54)

Rnd 9–12: sc in each st (54)

Rnd 13: hdc in FL of each st (54) **(see fig. 12c)**
- Finish off, weave in ends.

SHELL BOTTOM: Bright Green yarn
- ch 6, start in 2nd ch from hook.

Rnd 1: sc, 3sc, 3sc in next ch, 3sc, 2sc in next ch (12)

Rnd 2: *sc, 2sc in next st* (18)

Rnd 3: *2sc, 2sc in next st* (24)

Rnd 4: *3sc, 2sc in next st* (30)

Rnd 5: *4sc, 2sc in next st* (36) **(see fig. 12d)**

Rnd 6: *5sc, 2sc in next st* (42)

Rnd 7: *6sc, 2sc in next st* (48)

Rnd 8: *7sc, 2sc in next st* (54)
- Finish off, leaving a long tail to sew onto the shell top.

12d

12e

12f

LEGS (X4): Bright Green yarn

• Make an adjustable ring.

Rnd 1: 6sc in ring (6)

Rnd 2: 2sc in each st (12)

Rnd 3-9: sc in each st (12)

• Finish off, leaving a long tail to sew onto the shell.

HEAD: Bright Green yarn

• Make an adjustable ring.

Rnd 1: 6sc in ring (6)

Rnd 2: 2sc in each st (12)

Rnd 3: *sc, 2sc in next st* (18)

Rnd 4-7: sc in each st (18)

• Pause crocheting and attach safety eyes between rounds 4 and 5. **(see fig. 12e)**

Rnd 8: *sc, sc2tog* (12)

Rnd 9-12: sc in each st (12)

• Finish off, leaving a long tail to sew onto the shell.

FINISHING:

• Sew spots onto top of shell. **(see fig. 12f)**

• Partially stitch bottom of shell onto the top of the shell (using the front loops from round 13 of shell top), stuff shell with stuffing, finish stitching around and weave in ends. **(see fig. 12g)**

• Sew on head and legs to the bottom of the shell, weave in ends.

12g

71

About the Author

Kristen Rask opened Schmancy, a small shop specializing in art toys and collectibles in downtown Seattle, in 2004. Since the opening, she's received international attention for Plush You!, her annual show featuring plush artists from around the globe. Kristen is the author of numerous craft books including *Plush You! Loveable Misfits to Sew and Stuff* (2007), the *Creature Crochet* kit (2009), the *Yummy Crochet* kit (2011), *Teeny Tiny Animal Crochet* kit (2013), and the *Wizard of Oz Crochet* kit (2013).

Acknowledgments

I would like to thank first and foremost, the contributors to this book—all very talented people and so fun to work with! I would like to thank Dana Youlin and Emily Zach for making the process fun. Lastly my family and friends whom I would be nothing without.

Where to Find the Artists

Denise Ferguson's spirit animal is the cat. She has the amazing ability to take everyday items and animals and transform them, blending hilarity and a sweetly sinister touch. You can find her patterns at www.yummypancake.com.

Kandice Soraya Grote's spirit animal is the otter. Kandice splits her time working on her PhD and making irresistible amigurumi. She contributed projects to *Wizard of Oz Crochet* and *Teeny Tiny Animal Crochet*. You can find her work at www.etsy.com/shop/SpudsStitches.

Heather Jarmusz's spirit animal is the blue-footed booby. Heather's Bob's Burger's amigurumi pieces were featured in *Plush You!* You can find her work at www.hamandeggs.etsy.com.

Alicia Kachmar's spirit animal is the gibbon. In addition to making adorable amigurumi, Alicia is a writer and photographer. She contributed a project to *Yummy Crochet*. Find her ataliciakachmar.com.

Janene Scholz's spirit animal is the elephant. Janene sells adorable fuzzy creatures in her online shop. You can find perfect patterns for baby gifts and friends alike at www.etsy.com/shop/unclicheCrochet.

Rachelle Smith's spirit animal is the unicorn. Rachelle sells a plethora of adorable patterns as well as ready-made crochet friends at www.etsy.com/shop/yayhookdcrochet. You can also find one of her patterns in *Teeny Tiny Animal Crochet*.

Amanda Lynn Wilhite's spirit animal is the swan. Amanda sells everything from crochet accessories to toys in her online shop. You can also find one of her patterns in *Wizard of Oz Crochet*. Find her at www.indigocrochet.etsy.com.

becker&mayer!
BOOK PRODUCERS

becker&mayer! LLC
11120 NE 33rd Pl., Suite 101
Bellevue, WA 98004
www.beckermayer.com

© 2014 by becker&mayer! LLC

Designer: Sarah Baynes
Editor: Dana Youlin
Photographer: Joseph Lambert
Photo editor: Emily Zach
Production coordinator: Jennifer Marx
Product developer: Peter Schumacher

BM13630-16467

This book is part of the *Woodland Crochet* kit
and is not to be sold separately.

Design elements used throughout, via Shutterstock: Cardboard
background © pashabo; Faux wood pattern © ArtBitz; Leaf pattern
© Markovka/Shutterstock.

Manufactured in China

2 4 6 8 10 9 7 5 3